GREAT BIG ANIMAL book

by Ronne Randall

MAP KEY

GRASSLAND Dry areas covered with grass where only a few bushes and trees grow.

SAVANNAH (tropical grassland) Hot grassland with a few trees. At some times of the year they are very dry, and at other times there is lots of rain.

DESERT Large areas of very dry (normally sandy) land where hardly any rain falls. Only a few plants and animals live in the desert. It is very hot in the day and very cold at night.

TUNDRA Cold, windy places where the ground is always frozen. There are no trees, and no rain or snow.

ANTARCTIC (including South Pole) Frozen, snow-covered ground and icy seas. The coldest place on Earth! Hardly any plants live here, but lots of TOUGH animals – especially in the sea.

ARCTIC (including North Pole) Frozen, snow-covered ground and icy seas. Only a few TOUGH animals and plants live here!

TEMPERATE FOREST Cool, rainy forests where the trees lose their leaves in autumn and grow them back in spring.

CONIFEROUS FOREST Cold forests where coniferous trees grow (trees with needles and cones that stay green all year).

RAINFOREST Warm, wet forests where many animals live.

OCEAN Oceans cover almost ¾ of the Earth. Animals live in every bit of the ocean – even 11 kilometres down in the very deepest bits!

PACIFIC OCEAN

OCEANIA

LOOK for the maps throughout the book: they will tell you where in the world animals live!

Copyright © ticktock Entertainment Ltd 2005
First published in Great Britain in 2005 by ticktock Media Ltd.,
Unit 2, Orchard Business Centre, North Farm Road, Tunbridge Wells, Kent, TN2 3XF

We would like to thank: Duncan Bolton at Bristol Zoo; the Entomology Department and the Bird Group (Department of Zoology) at The Natural History Museum, London; Isolde McGeorge at Chester Zoo and Elizabeth Wiggans.

With special thanks to Lorna Cowan and Caroline Martin.

ISBN 1 86007 837 0 pbk
Printed in China

CONTENTS

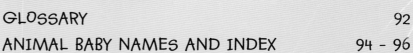

INTRODUCTION

Welcome to the **GREAT BIG ANIMAL BOOK!** It's packed with strange and wonderful creatures from EVERY corner of the world – some you will know REALLY well, and others you may not have seen before!

Did you know that there are almost 2 million different kinds of animals on Earth?

MAMMAL

All the animals in this book have been divided into five different groups:

MAMMALS, BIRDS, REPTILES and **AMPHIBIANS, UNDERWATER CREATURES** (including fish) and **BUGS AND SPIDERS.**

A furry coat

Most <u>mammals</u> give birth to live babies, and then feed them with milk from their own bodies. They mostly have furry or hairy coats, too! <u>Birds</u> are egg-laying animals with feathers.

REPTILE

<u>Reptiles</u> are creatures with thick, scaly skins. Most reptiles lay eggs, but some give birth to live babies. <u>Amphibians</u> are animals that live part of the time in water and part of the time on land, while <u>fish (and the other underwater creatures)</u> live in water all of the time. <u>Bugs and spiders</u> live just about everywhere!

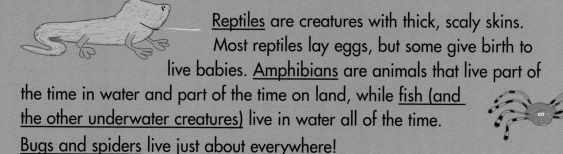

Mammals and birds are <u>warm-blooded</u>. This means their body temperature stays the same no matter how hot or cold the air, or water, is around them. Bugs, spiders, reptiles, amphibians and fish are all <u>cold-blooded</u>. Their body temperature goes up and down depending on how hot or cold their surroundings are.

A thick, scaly skin

DO ALL ANIMALS EAT THE SAME STUFF?

Some animals, like lions or sharks, only eat meat or fish – they are called **carnivores** (you will see the symbol on the right next to their names). Others, like reindeer and elephants, only eat plants – they are called **herbivores**. Some animals, like grizzly bears and racoons, eat plants and meat (or fish) – they are called **omnivores**.

Symbols to look out for :

 = carnivore

 = herbivore

 = omnivore

SOME BAD NEWS

Many of the world's wild animals are **endangered**. Sometimes it is because too many of them have been killed by hunters, or because they have been captured by people who want to sell them as unusual pets. Often it is because the places where they live, their habitats, have been destroyed. People chop down rainforest trees so that they can sell the wood, and farmers dig up the land where wild animals live to grow food for their own families.

Endangered orang-utan

SOME GOOD NEWS

There are ways to help endangered animals though – this is called conservation. Many governments have passed laws that ban hunting, and in some countries special parks have been created where endangered animals can live in safety.

People are animals, too. We are mammals – just like our cousins the apes. It is up to us to help look after our world and ALL the animals we share it with!

Now turn the page to see some COOL creatures...

Any words that look bold, **like this**, are explained in the glossary on pages 92 – 93.

BIG CATS

with really BIG teeth!

Cats have amazing eyesight and hearing. They are **carnivores**, so they only eat meat. Their coats can be striped or spotted, helping them to hide. This is called **camouflage**.

CHEETAH

Big cats play, too!

Cheetahs use their long tails for balance while they are running.

Over short distances cheetahs can run at more than 100 km/h! They are the world's fastest land animal.

After chasing and killing its **prey**, the cheetah needs about 30 minutes to get its breath back before it can eat.

TIGER

Tigers are the biggest cats of all. They are so strong, they can kill and eat a whole deer!

6

ROAR!

Tigers love to cool off in the water and are excellent swimmers.

Time for a bath!

Each tiger has its own special pattern of stripes. Like human fingerprints, the stripes are all different.

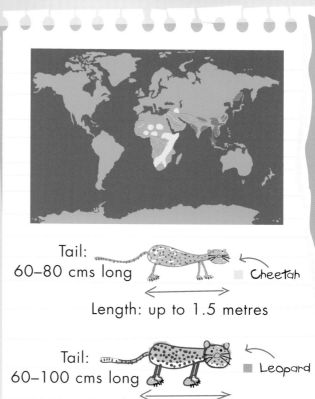

Tail: 60–80 cms long — Cheetah
Length: up to 1.5 metres

Tail: 60–100 cms long — Leopard
Length: up to 1.9 metres

Tail: up to 1 metre long — Tiger
Length: up to 3 metres

 LEOPARD

Leopards can jump 4 metres high without even trying!

They are very good at climbing, and will often hide their food in trees.

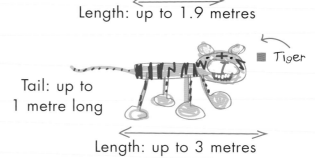
Time to relax

Some leopards are very dark, they are known as black panthers. It is hard to see their spots, but they are still there!

Spot the spots!

7

LIONS

Lions live in family groups called 'prides'. They are the only big cats who live in groups as adults. Prides normally have about four to six adult members. All the females in a pride are related, and they help to look after each other's babies.

LION

Most of the world's lions live on the grasslands of Africa.

Baby lions are called cubs.

When male cubs are about 18 months old, they start to grow a thick mane of hair around their head.

8

Lions are the only cats with manes and tufts at the end of their tails.

Look at those teeth!

IMPORTANT NOTE

The Asiatic lion **is endangered** and now only lives in the Gir Forest National Park in India. There are fewer than **300 left!**

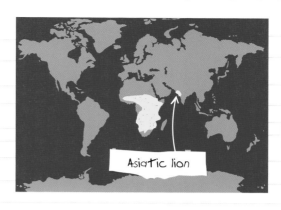

Asiatic lion

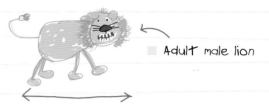

Adult male lion

Length: up to 3 metres (including tail)
Weight: up to 240 kilograms

Adult female lioness

Length: 2.5 metres (including tail)
Weight: up to 180 kilograms

Lion language is made up of lots of different growls: from low, rumbly grumbles to mighty ROARS that can be heard up to 8 kilometres away!

Grrrrrr

LIONESS

Lionesses don't have manes.

Lions will hunt anything from hares to hippos, but their main **prey** is antelope, zebra and buffalo.

Lions spend a lot of time sleeping. They snooze for up to 20 hours each day.

Lions can't run for long distances, they usually creep up on their prey and then POUNCE on them! Lions hunt as a team, but the lionesses do most of the work.

9

THE DOG FAMILY

Wolves, foxes and pet dogs are all members of the same family. In the wild, dogs and wolves live in groups called 'packs'. A male and female pair leads the pack, and they are the only pair to have puppies. All members of the dog family have a very good **sense** of smell which helps them find food.

SNIFF! SNIFF!

Picking up the scent.

Bloodhounds' noses are 60 times more powerful than other dogs', and a million times more powerful than yours!

Bloodhounds can follow scents in heavy rain, and in temperatures below zero or as high as 37°C.

BLOODHOUND

Domestic dogs have been trained by humans to herd other animals, guard buildings, rescue people and even do police work!

Bloodhounds can help the police track lost people. Their sense of smell is so good, they can smell a person's scent from fingerprints on a drink can.

10

GREY WOLF

Large, sensitive ears

Most wolves live in cold places. To keep warm, they have a thick coat made up of two types of hair – a woolly undercoat and an outer layer of guard hairs.

Wolves howl to each other to keep in touch, using a pack song. The sound of their howls can travel for miles.

HOWL

Hunting as a pack, wolves can catch large **prey**, such as reindeer and even moose.

Pet and working dogs live all over the world!

Grey wolf

Height: 90 centimetres (to the shoulder)

Bloodhound

Height: 63.5 centimetres (to the shoulder)

Red fox

Height: 50 centimetres (to the shoulder)

RED FOX

Red foxes used to live in woodlands, but now there are more of them living in towns than in the countryside. They raid rubbish bins in search of food.

Foxes eat rabbits, birds, mice, beetles, frogs, fruit – in fact, almost anything!

A bushy tail called a BRUSH

The red fox is the largest of all the foxes.

11

ANIMALS WITH POUCHES

Animals with pouches are called **marsupials**. They give birth to very, very, tiny babies that are blind and have no hair. Marsupial babies crawl into their mother's pouch where they feed and grow, until they are big enough to go out into the world!

Mostly from Australia

RED KANGAROO

The red kangaroo is the largest of all the marsupials. They live in family groups called 'mobs'.

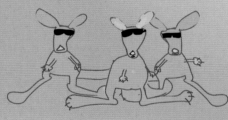

Kangaroos move by hopping on their big, powerful back legs, using their tails for balance. They can move at over 50 km/h!

Hi mum!

The joey (baby kangaroo) stays in mum's pouch for about six to eleven months!

During the daytime, when it's hot, kangaroos sleep in the shade; but in the cooler, late afternoon and evening, they come out to eat their favourite food – grass.

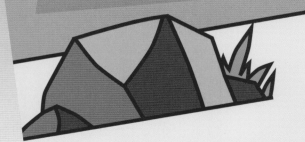

TASMANIAN DEVIL

The Tasmanian devil's powerful jaws and sharp teeth can completely crunch up birds and little animals, like possums – even the bones and fur!

They hunt at night!

They were given the name 'DEVIL' by people who were frightened by their snarling barks and high-pitched shrieks.

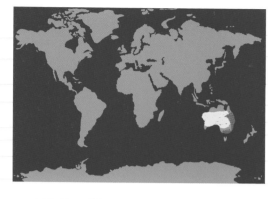

→ Red kangaroo

Height: up to 1.7 metres

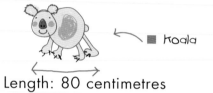

→ koala

Length: 80 centimetres

→ Tasmanian devil

Length: up to 80 centimetres

KOALA

Koalas live in trees – eucalyptus trees are their favourite! They mostly feed at night and will eat up to 500 grams of eucalyptus leaves during their nightly feast.

The koala's habitat is now in danger! The trees where they live are being cut down to make room for farms, roads and buildings.

Their diet of eucalyptus makes koalas smell like cough drops!

Koala paws are especially good for gripping and climbing. Koalas even sleep up in the treetops.

13

APES

Apes belong to an animal family called **primates**. People are primates too, and apes are our closest animal relatives. Apes even look a bit like us, but they are MUCH hairier!

ORANG-UTAN

Orang-utans live in rainforests. Their name means 'man of the forest'.

Arms can span over 2 metres!

They have very long, strong arms – just right for swinging through the treetops, looking for fruit.

Gorillas are the biggest of all the primates. An adult male (like this one) can weigh up to 200 kilograms.

IMPORTANT NOTE
Because of habitat loss and hunting, gorillas, orang-utans and chimpanzees are all now seriously endangered.

Adult orang-utans live on their own. Each night they make a new nest of leaves and branches to sleep in.

GORILLA

Gorillas live in family groups of up to 20 members. They search for food together. They eat leaves, plant stems and shoots, roots and fruit.

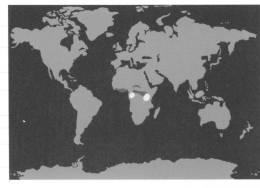

Each family is led by an adult male. He protects the females and babies, and is called a 'silverback'.

The hair on a male gorilla's back turns a silver colour when he is about ten years old.

Gorilla — Height: up to 1.7 metres

Orang-utan — Height: up to 1.37 metres

Chimpanzee — Height: up to 90 centimetres

CHIMPANZEE

Clever chimpanzees can use tools. They poke sticks into termite nests, then pull them out and lick off the tasty termites.

Chimps live in BIG groups.

Found anything tasty?

Gorillas make a kind of barking cough when they're upset and a purring 'mmmm' sound when they're happy.

Chimpanzees mainly eat fruit, leaves and seeds, but sometimes they hunt for birds and small monkeys! In captivity, chimps can live to be over 50 years old.

MONKEYS

Very clever, with good memories!

Monkeys walk on all fours.

Monkeys are **primates**, just like apes and people. You can tell monkeys and apes apart because apes don't have tails, but most monkeys do.

SNOW MONKEY

Snow monkeys actually make little balls of snow with their hands then roll them along the ground to make snowballs! Some snow monkeys warm up in pools of water that are heated by hot, underground springs.

Snow monkeys (or Japanese macaques) live in 'troops' of 20 to 30 animals in the forests and mountains of Japan.

16

MANDRILL

Males have colourful faces and a purple bottom! This makes them very handsome to female mandrills.

The BIGGEST monkey of all!

Red nose day!

During the day, noisy groups of mandrills search for food on the ground like fruit, seeds, eggs and small creatures. At night they sleep in trees.

A mandrill's cheek pouches can hold a whole bellyful of food, leaving their feet and hands free for running.

Snow monkeys eat leaves and flowers in spring, fruit in autumn and tree buds and bark in winter. They will also eat crabs and grasshoppers!

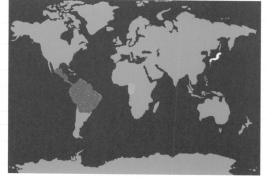

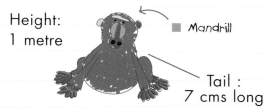

Height: 1 metre

■ Mandrill

Tail : 7 cms long

Height: 60 centimetres

Snow monkey

Thick, furry coat

Tail : 10 cms long

■ Capuchin monkey

Tail : 50 cms long

Length: 45 centimetres

CAPUCHIN MONKEY

Good at climbing trees

Capuchin monkeys live in the rainforest treetops. They only come down to the ground to drink. Their strong, bendy tails can hold on to branches and help them keep their balance.

Capuchins eat fruit, seeds and nuts, but they also like to eat **insects**, spiders, oysters and even tree frogs! They live in groups of 8 to 14.

17

BEARS

Bears are big, heavy, shaggy-coated mammals. Their eyesight and hearing are not very good, but with their large snouts, they have an excellent **sense** of smell.

GIANT PANDA

GRIZZLY BEAR

The giant panda is one of the world's most **endangered** animals. There are fewer than 1000 left in the world.

Baby pandas are pink and hairless when they are born. They only weigh about 100 grams – mum can weigh over 100 kilograms!

When a grizzly bear stands up on its back legs it can be 3.5 metres tall! They do this to threaten enemies and to look for food.

18

Pandas eat bamboo, a kind of tough, woody grass.

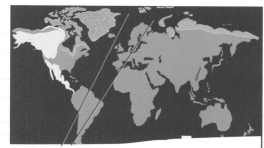

Over short distances grizzly bears can run at about 56 km/h!

Grizzly bears are a type of brown bear. They can be fierce if they feel they are in danger, but are usually peaceful and like to be left alone.

Salmon for dinner!

They mostly eat plants, but will also eat meat – especially fish. In winter they snuggle down to sleep in a den until spring. This is called **hibernation**.

When the Arctic Ocean freezes in winter, polar bears live and hunt on the frozen sea.

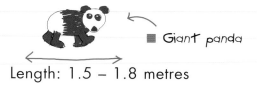

Giant panda
Length: 1.5 – 1.8 metres

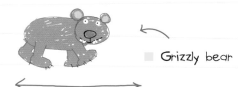

Grizzly bear
Length: up to 2.5 metres

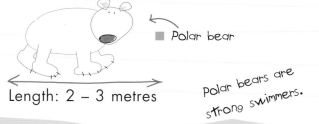

Polar bear
Length: 2 – 3 metres

Polar bears are strong swimmers.

POLAR BEAR

Polar bears are the biggest, land-living **carnivores** in the world. They hunt for seals and walruses in the sea and on the ice.

Thick, warm fur

Polar bear paws have furry pads for gripping the ice and they are **webbed** for swimming.

Polar bear fur looks white, which is good **camouflage** on the ice – but each hair is actually a see-through, hollow tube. The clear hairs reflect the sun's light. This is what makes polar bears look white!

19

SMALL SWIMMING ANIMALS

Animals that spend most of their time in the water are called **aquatic**. They have thick, waterproof fur to keep them warm in the water, and **webbed** feet to help them swim.

They have duck-like feet!

AMERICAN BEAVER

Beaver families live in homes called 'lodges', built from sticks held together with mud.

They use their strong teeth to cut down trees for building dams (large barriers) in the streams where they live.

A flat, scaly tail

Water builds up behind the dam creating a protective moat around the lodge and a safe, underwater place for storing tasty branches.

SEA OTTER

Sea otters enjoy shellfish like clams. Holding a rock on their chest, they float on their back and crack open the shell on the rock!

Platypuses live alone.

PLATYPUS

When the first platypus was brought to England from Australia two hundred years ago, people thought it was a made-up animal.

No one could believe a real animal could have a bill and webbed feet like a duck, and fur and a tail like a beaver.

The platypus lays eggs, like a bird or reptile, but feeds its babies milk because it is a mammal. Adults eat crayfish, worms, snails and shrimp.

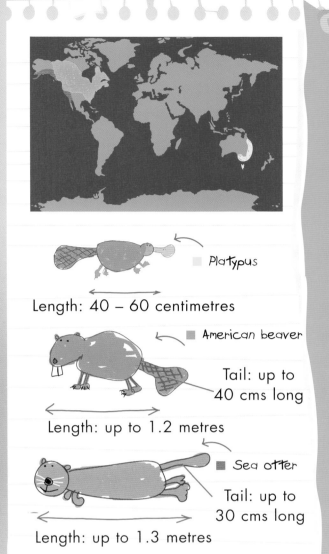

Platypus

Length: 40 – 60 centimetres

American beaver

Tail: up to 40 cms long

Length: up to 1.2 metres

Sea otter

Tail: up to 30 cms long

Length: up to 1.3 metres

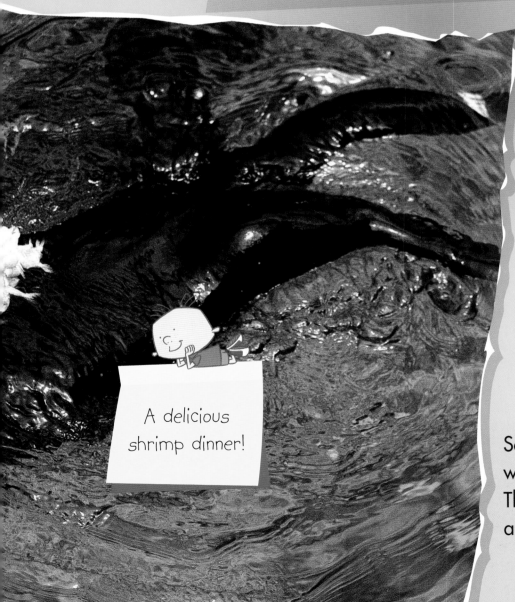

A delicious shrimp dinner!

Sea otters love to groom each other. They have the animal Kingdom's thickest fur.

Sometimes before sea otters go to sleep they wrap themselves in kelp (a type of seaweed). This keeps them in once place and stops them drifting out to sea!

21

SPIKY ANIMALS

Porcupines and hedgehogs both have spiny coats, which help protect them from **predators**. They look alike, but are different in lots of ways.

Have ~~twills~~ ~~ewills~~ quills

HEDGEHOG

Hedgehogs have whiskers and long snouts which help them find the **insects**, slugs and worms that they love to eat.

A scared hedgehog curls up into a tight, spiky ball – making it very difficult for an enemy to attack it!

Their thick, spiny coat has up to 7000 spines.

This looks cosy!

During winter some hedgehogs that live in cold places have trouble finding food. They snuggle under piles of dead leaves and **hibernate** until springtime.

22

PORCUPINE

Porcupines can have up to 30,000 quills.
When they lose one a new one grows in its place.

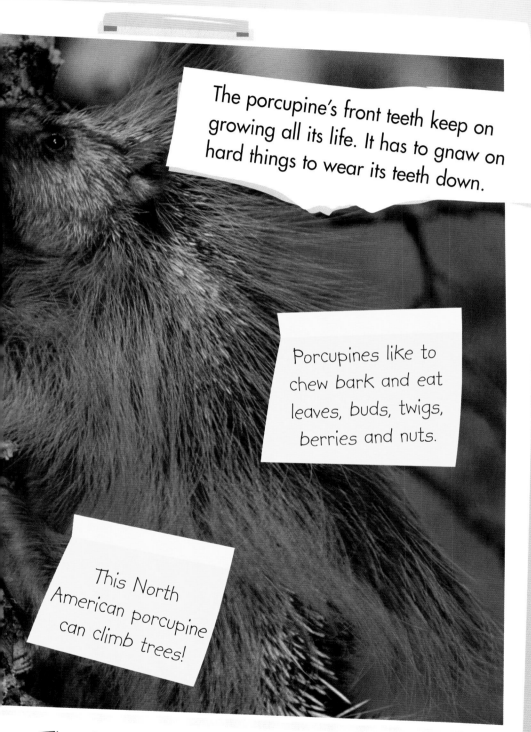

The porcupine's front teeth keep on growing all its life. It has to gnaw on hard things to wear its teeth down.

Porcupines like to chew bark and eat leaves, buds, twigs, berries and nuts.

This North American porcupine can climb trees!

The Cape porcupine, from Africa, shelters in caves and in crevices (gaps) in rocks.

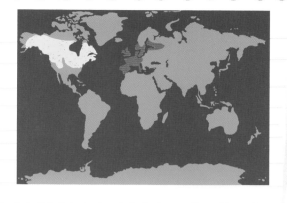

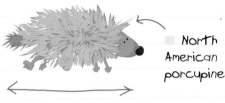

North American porcupine

Length: up to 86 centimetres

Western European hedgehog

Length: 22 – 27 centimetres

Porcupines have a woolly undercoat and an outer coat of soft guard hairs between their spiky quills.

When a porcupine gets scared, its quills stand up on end. The quills can be dangerous – if they pierce the skin, it is very difficult to get them out.

So if you see a porcupine, don't frighten it and don't get too close!

23

SEALS, SEA LIONS and others

Mammals that spend most of their time in the sea are called **marine** mammals. Manatees stay in the water all the time, while seals, sea lions and walruses spend some time out of the water.

Love swimming and sunbathing!

SEA LION

California sea lions are clever and very playful! They can use their flippers to move about on land.

Sea lions gather on land in groups called 'colonies'. Fish and squid are their favourite foods.

Sea lions have short, stubbly hair rather than fur.

seafood takeaway

Favourite food is fish, fish and more fish!

WALRUS

Male walruses have long **tusks** that are actually teeth. The tusks can grow up to 1 metre long.

Walruses can stay underwater for 25 minutes! They use their tusks to root around on the seabed for shellfish, snails and worms.

Walruses use their tusks to help pull themselves out of the water. This is very useful as a male walrus can weigh 2 tonnes!

24

SEAL

Some seal pups born in icy, snowy places like the Arctic have white fur to **camouflage** them.

A harp seal pup

Seals like to laze in the sun, but are clumsy when they move on land or ice. In the water they are fast and graceful.

Many seals live in cold water. Thick fur and a layer of **blubber** keep them warm.

MANATEE

Manatees are gentle, slow-moving animals. They eat lots and lots of underwater plants.

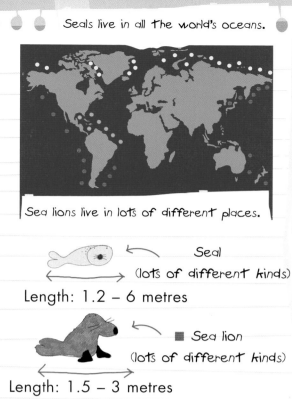

Seals live in all the world's oceans.

Sea lions live in lots of different places.

Seal
(lots of different kinds)
Length: 1.2 – 6 metres

Sea lion
(lots of different kinds)
Length: 1.5 – 3 metres

Walrus
Length: 3.5 metres

Manatee
(West Indian)
Length: up to 4.5 metres

There are lots of old stories of sailors seeing mermaids. Nowadays some people think that the creatures the sailors saw were actually manatees, who live close to the shore in shallow water.

Many manatees are covered in scars where they have been hit by boats. They are also in danger from fishing nets and polluted water.

25

DOLPHINS AND WHALES

Whales and dolphins belong to a family called **cetaceans.** They are mammals so they don't have **gills** (like fish) and need to come above water to breathe through **blowholes** on the top of their heads. They speak to each other in whistles, groans and squeaks.

Feed their babies milk!

BLUE WHALE

The blue whale is the biggest creature ever to have lived on Earth – it weighs the same as 20 elephants!

No teeth!

A heart the size of a VW beetle!

The blue whale is also the loudest animal on Earth. Its whistle-like call is louder than a jet plane.

Blue whales can eat up to 4000 kilograms of **plankton** (tiny sea plants and creatures) in a day. They suck in gallons of water then sieve out the food through special, bristly parts of their mouths called baleen plates.

BOTTLENOSE DOLPHIN

Bottle-shaped beak

Bottlenose dolphins are actually small whales. They eat fish and shellfish.

Dolphins will chase a school of fish, circling nearer and nearer until the fish form a huge ball-shaped crowd. Then the dolphins dive into the middle to snap up a tasty meal!

Clever dolphins talk to each other using sounds and signs, such as slapping the water with their tails. They can leap into the air as high as 6 metres!

Blue whales, orcas and bottlenose dolphins live in all the world's oceans.

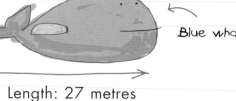

Blue whale

Length: 27 metres

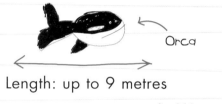

Orca

Length: up to 9 metres

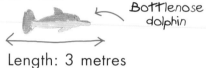

Bottlenose dolphin

Length: 3 metres

ORCA (KILLER WHALE)

See any seafood?

Orcas live in family groups called pods. Each pod has its own special language.

The male orca's dorsal fin can be 1.8 metres high.

Besides eating squid and shrimp, orcas are excellent hunters – they attack birds, seals, other whales and even sharks!

Their dark backs **camouflage** them in the water.

27

HIPPOS AND RHINOS

Rhinos and hippos both look a bit fierce, but they actually only eat plants – not other animals. Still, they will attack anyone who threatens them, and hippos are one of the most dangerous animals in Africa!

Huge and very HEAVY

HIPPOPOTAMUS

Hippopotamus means 'river horse' in ancient Greek (a language from long ago).

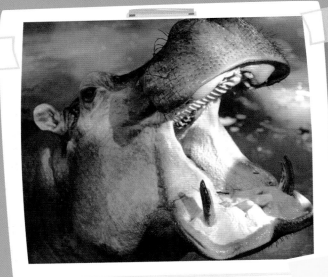

Open wide!

Hippos have ENORMOUS teeth that keep growing all their lives. Males use their teeth when they are fighting over females.

Hippos spend almost all day in the water lazing around and eating water plants. At night they come out onto land and graze on grass and reeds.

Hippo sweat is pink or red. It contains special substances to cool the hippo down and keep its skin healthy.

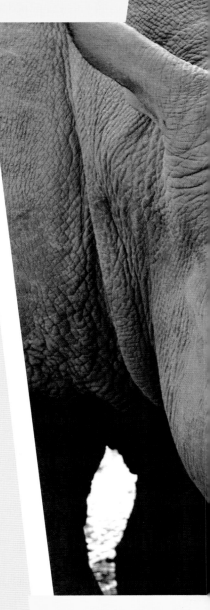

Rhinos need to eat massive amounts of grass, twigs and leaves every day.

28

RHINOCEROS

There are five different kinds of rhino – white, black, Indian, Sumatran and Javan.

Rhinos have bad eyesight, but a good **sense** of smell and good hearing.

Rhino horns are made of a tough material called keratin mixed with hair. Keratin is in your hair and fingernails, too.

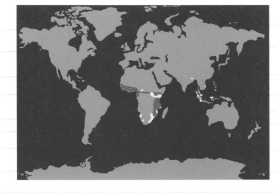

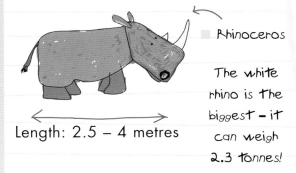

Rhinoceros

The white rhino is the biggest – it can weigh 2.3 tonnes!

Length: 2.5 – 4 metres

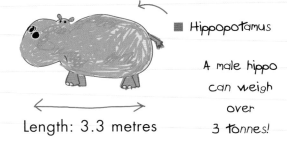

Hippopotamus

A male hippo can weigh over 3 tonnes!

Length: 3.3 metres

CHARGE!

Look out!

IMPORTANT NOTE

So many rhinos have been killed for their horns that they are now **endangered**. People kill them because they falsely believe that crushed rhino horn can cure illnesses. Rhinos are also losing their habitat as humans move in to the areas where they live.

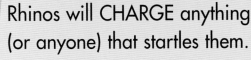

Rhinos will CHARGE anything (or anyone) that startles them.

29

ELEPHANTS

Elephants are the largest animal that lives on land. There are three different kinds – African savannah elephants, African forest elephants and Asian elephants. African elephants are slightly larger than Asian and have much bigger ears.

Grass for lunch again

Elephants live on savannahs and in forests. They can eat up to 200 kilograms of bark, leaves, branches and grass every day.

Elephants' trunks are not just noses. They use them to pull down trees, pick up food, suck up water and spray protective dust over their backs when they get hot.

The tip of an elephant's trunk is very sensitive. It can even pick up a feather from the ground.

Elephants cannot run or jump, but they can walk very fast.

Elephants can live as long as 70 years!

Anyone fancy a paddle?

Elephants drink almost 200 litres of water a day – enough to fill a bathtub!

They are good swimmers, and can use their trunks like snorkels.

Elephant herds are made up of related females and their babies. When males grow up, they leave the herd.

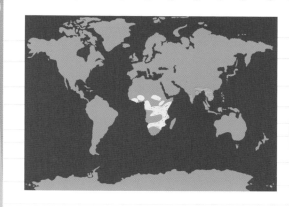

Height: up to 3.5 metres (to the shoulder)

African elephant

Weight: 4 – 6 tonnes

Height: 2.75 metres (to the shoulder)

Asian elephant

Weight: up to 5.5 tonnes

Baby elephants suck their trunks.

IMPORTANT NOTE

Adult elephants only have one enemy – humans! For many years they were killed for their tusks, but this is now against the law. However, elephants are still in danger. More and more humans are moving into the areas where they live and elephants are losing their habitats.

Elephants are good mums and aunties. They will crook their trunk around a baby's bottom to help it climb a steep hill, and shelter it from hot sun under their bodies. All the members of a herd will protect a baby from **predators**.

31

GIRAFFES AND CAMELS

Camels and giraffes both have special stomachs that let them chew up their food, swallow it and then when it is in their stomach, burp it back up and eat it all over again – to get maximum nutrition (goodness) out of it!

GIRAFFE

Hundreds of years ago, the Romans called giraffes 'camelopards'. They thought they were camels with leopard spots.

Amazing patterns!

Their long legs, neck and tongue help giraffes reach leaves at the tops of trees. A giraffe's tongue can be 45 centimetres long!

Giraffes can eat up to 63.5 kilograms of leaves a day.

When giraffe calves are born, they are already nearly 2 metres tall – the same height as a man!

Eat leaves and bushes

Giraffes are the tallest animals in the world.

32

DROMEDARY

One hump only

Camels survive by storing fat in their humps which gives them energy.

There are two types of camel – dromedaries and Bactrian camels. They both live in places where there is normally not much food or water, such as deserts and mountains.

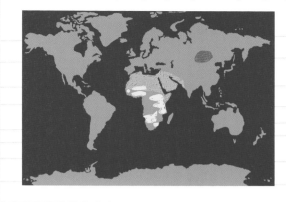

Giraffe   Dromedary

Height: up to 2.3 metres (to top of hump)

Bactrian camel

Height: up to 5.3 metres

Height: up to 2.3 metres (to top of humps)

BACTRIAN CAMEL

Camels can go for almost two weeks without water, then drink up to 100 litres in one go – to top up again!

Two humps

Camels have two rows of eyelashes to protect their eyes during sandstorms. Their nostrils can also be closed to keep out sand.

Bactrian camels have a shaggy coat.

FARM ANIMALS...

Animals such as cows, goats and pigs are kept on farms. They give us milk and meat. We also use their skin for leather and their woolly coats for making cloth.

WILD BOAR

COW

A cow (mum)

Dad is called a bull.

Cows eat grass and chew their cud (food that they have already eaten and burped back up) for up to eight hours every day!

Before she can start producing milk, a cow must have a calf (a baby).

YAK

People who live in Tibet get milk and meat from yaks. They use yak skins to make tents, and their hair to make rugs and ropes.

Yaks are shaggy, mountain cousins of cows.

Yaks eat grass, moss and herbs. If there is no water high up in the mountains, they crunch up ice.

GOAT

There are many different types of goats. Some live on farms and others are wild.

Angora goats hav hair that can be made into a soft, si wool called 'mohair

34

PIG

Farm pigs and wild boars are cousins.

Lives in a farm pen.

Farm cows, goats and pigs live all over the world.

Wild boars live in forests and have hairy, bristly coats. They are fast runners and good at swimming.

Their long snouts and **tusks** help them dig up the plant roots and bulbs they like to eat.

Yak

Height: 1 – 2 metres (to the shoulder)

Cow

Height: 1.5 metres (to the shoulder)

Farm goat

Height: up to 1 metre (to the shoulder)

Ibex

Height: 90 centimetres (to the shoulder)

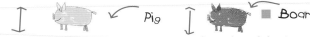

Pig

Boar

Height: 90 centimetres (to the shoulder)

IBEX

Goats can live in deserts or up high mountains because they don't mind eating the scrubby plants that grow in these tough places.

A dairy (milking) goat

Good climbers

Ibex are wild mountain goats that live in herds. They can climb quickly to avoid wolves and bears. They use their horns to fight them off, too.

35

HORSES AND ZEBRAS

Just one toe on each foot!

Horses and zebras both have long legs that help them run fast over long distances. People tamed horses more than 5000 years ago, but zebras are still wild. Horses and zebras both eat grass, but tame horses have hay (dried grass) and get extra treats like carrots and apples!

HORSE

Male horses (and zebras) are known as stallions. Females are called mares, and their babies are called foals.

Foals can stand up and walk just an hour or two after they are born!

ZEBRA

They live in family groups made up of a stallion and several mares and their foals.

Zebras live on the African grasslands.

A zebra foal

Good **camouflage**

To **predators** like lions, who are colour blind, the zebra's stripes blend in with the tall grass, so the zebra becomes almost invisible!

Sometimes zebras join herds of antelope and they all help one another look out for predators.

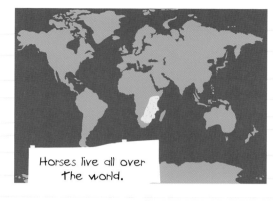

Horses live all over the world.

Horse

Height: 1.5 metres or 15 hands (to the shoulder)
*ponies are 1.4 metres or less

Zebra

Height: 1.35 metres (to the shoulder)

A stallion

Horses normally sleep standing up, but they will lie down if they feel safe.

Horses' hooves are always growing, like our fingernails. Horses used for riding or work have their hooves trimmed. They also wear protective metal shoes on the bottom of their hooves.

Horses are measured in 'hands'. One hand is 10 centimetres, about the width of a grown-up's hand.

37

ANIMALS WITH HORNS

Deer and antelope are cousins. Adult male deer have bony **antlers** on their heads. The antlers fall off every year, and then grow again. In the antelope world, both males and females have horns, which keep growing all their lives.

Good at head-butting

MOOSE

Moose like being near water. They will often wade into lakes to eat underwater plants.

When deer antlers are growing they are covered with soft skin called velvet. It gets rubbed off on trees and in fights.

HUGE antlers

Moose are the biggest deer in the world. In Europe they are called elk.

REINDEER

In summer, reindeer eat grasses and herbs. In winter they use their hooves to dig under the snow to find fungus and moss to eat.

Reindeer are the only deer where both males and females have antlers.

People tamed reindeer about 7000 years ago, but there are still many wild reindeer, too.

Domestic (tame) reindeer pull sledges and are kept for their meat and skins.

Anyone see Rudolph?

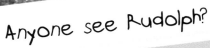

The reindeer's thick coat keeps out the Arctic cold.

Lots of different antelope come from Africa.

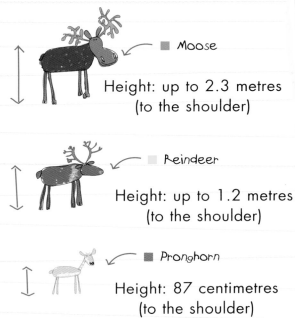

■ Moose

Height: up to 2.3 metres (to the shoulder)

Reindeer

Height: up to 1.2 metres (to the shoulder)

 ■ Pronghorn

Height: 87 centimetres (to the shoulder)

PRONGHORN

The pronghorn has horns like an antelope, but it sheds them every year, like a deer!

Pronghorns can run at 70 km/h and jump up to 6 metres in one leap.

ANTELOPE

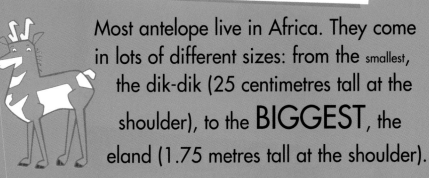

Most antelope live in Africa. They come in lots of different sizes: from the smallest, the dik-dik (25 centimetres tall at the shoulder), to the BIGGEST, the eland (1.75 metres tall at the shoulder).

Antelope horns can be long, short, twisted, curved or straight.

39

ANIMALS WITH FANCY TAILS

The bushy, striped tails of these animals make them easy to see in the forests where they live. A raised tail is a signal to friends, and warns enemies to keep away!

RACCOON

Nocturnal raccoons live in forests, but often come into towns to steal food from rubbish bins.

They eat everything from insects, nuts and berries to fish and frogs. With their skilful paws they can even turn on water taps and open cans of fizzy drink!

A mask like a bandit!

Raccoons often wash dirt off their food before eating it.

Ring-tailed lemurs spend time in trees and on the ground. They also love to sunbathe.

RING-TAILED LEMUR

Groups of ring-tailed lemurs can travel up to 6 kilometres a day searching for food. They eat fruit, leaves, birds' eggs and small animals.

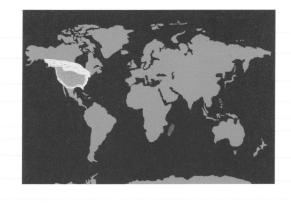

When fighting over females, males rub their tails on special **scent glands** on their wrists. Then they have 'stink fights' by flicking their tails at one another.

■ Ring-tailed lemur — Tail: 60 cms long
Length: 44 centimetres

■ Raccoon (common) — Tail: 25 cms long
Length: up to 60 centimetres

Striped — Tail: 25 cms long
Length: up to 75 centimetres

SKUNK

Skunks are best known for the nasty smell they give off. If an enemy is nearby skunks stamp their feet then do a warning handstand.

If the enemy doesn't move away, they spray a smelly liquid out of their bottoms – it can reach as far as 3 metres!

Skunks love to eat people's leftovers!

41

ODD-LOOKING ANIMALS

These curious creatures may look strange to us, but their bodies are perfect for the places where they live. The sloth's big claws are just right for hanging in trees, and the anteater's long snout is great for slurping up insects!

ANTEATER

Anteaters have long, tube-like snouts that are good at smelling out ant and termite nests.

Their strong, sharp claws rip the ant and termite nests apart, then their sticky tongues lap up the insects.

A giant anteater can eat up to 30,000 ants and termites a day.

The giant anteater lives on the ground, but the silky anteater lives in trees, and eats tree ants.

This busy tongue is 60 centimetres long!

SLOTH

Sloths hang upside-down in rainforest trees, using their curved claws to hold on.

Green fur?

A sloth's favourite food is leaves – so everything it needs is up in the treetops!

Camouflage is important, because sloths move very slowly and are easily caught by **predators**.

Some sloths even have green **algae** (types of plants) growing in their coats, this helps to camouflage them.

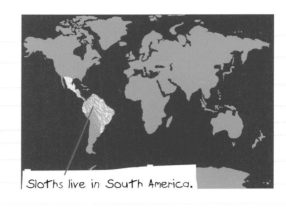

Sloths live in South America.

Giant anteater

Length: 2 metres (including tail)

Sloth

Height: 65 centimetres

Nine-banded armadillo

Length: 57 centimetres (including tail)

ARMADILLO

Armadillo means 'armoured' in Spanish. Bony armour protects the armadillo from enemies.

It has a long, sticky tongue for slurping up insects.

A nine-banded armadillo

Nine-banded armadillos are good swimmers, and even walk along the bottoms of streams and ponds – underwater!

43

FLYING ANIMALS

Bats are the only mammals that have wings, and can actually fly. (Flying squirrels <u>look</u> as if they are flying, but they are really gliding.)

They are mammals not birds!

BATS

FLYING SQUIRREL

The North American flying squirrel can leap off a high tree branch and then glide downwards and along for over 50 metres – landing in the lower branches of another tree.

Flying squirrels eat acorns, nuts, berries and seeds.

They have a flap of skin that joins the front and back legs – like a sort of parachute. They steer and change direction by turning their legs and flapping their tails.

44

Flying squirrels are **nocturnal**. Their big eyes are good for seeing in the dark.

Bats live in **colonies** in trees, holes in rocks, buildings or caves.

During the day they hang upside-down to sleep. At night they fly out to look for food.

Most bats eat **insects**. When hunting, the bats make high-pitched sounds. This is called echolocation. Echoes from the sounds bounce off the insects telling the bats where to find them.

This is a leaf nose bat!

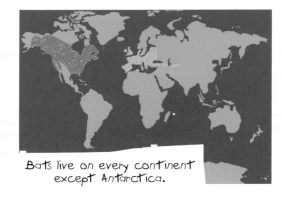

Bats live on every continent except Antarctica.

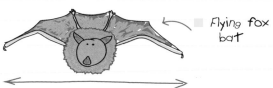

Flying fox bat

1.7 metres (wing tip to wing tip)

Flying squirrel (North American)

Length: 30 – 40 centimetres (including tail)

Pipistrelle bat (common)

25 centimetres (wing tip to wing tip)

A flying fox bat

The vampire bat lives on blood. It makes small holes in other mammals and birds with its two sharp teeth, then laps up their blood!

The flying fox is a type of fruit bat. They find fruit by using their **sense** of smell – they like to eat the soft, juicy middle bits best!

45

FAST-MOVING ANIMALS

These animals are very good at getting away from their enemies. They either run or hop away very fast, or escape into their underground homes. All these animals eat grass and plants.

Some rabbits live in large groups in underground **burrows**.

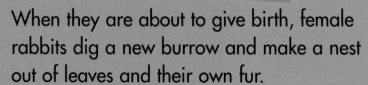

RABBIT

When they are about to give birth, female rabbits dig a new burrow and make a nest out of leaves and their own fur.

Any danger?

The babies, called kittens, are born blind with no fur.

Rabbits stay close to their burrow so they can quickly escape from enemies.

JACK RABBIT

Jack rabbits are really a type of hare. They live above ground, and have their babies in a simple nest called a 'form'.

Hares are bigger and thinner than rabbits.

Strong back legs

Hares can run very fast and leap 1.5 metres in the air.

Jack rabbits have black tips on their ears.

Hares have longer ears and longer back legs than rabbits.

46

PRAIRIE DOG

Prairie dogs live in underground burrows that are connected to form 'towns'.

Sometimes prairie dogs look like they're kissing – they are really trying to recognize their friends by smell.

They disappear into their burrows at the first sign of danger.

Rabbits live on every continent except Antarctica.

Jack rabbit

Length: 50 – 60 centimetres

Rabbit

Length: up to 50 centimetres

Prairie dog

Length: 30 – 40 centimetres

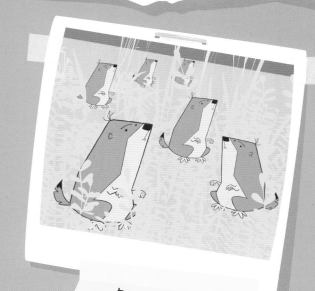

Prairie dog towns can stretch for miles!

47

ANIMALS WITH BIG FRONT TEETH

These little animals were all born to gnaw – bite and chew on things! Their big, strong, front teeth keep growing and growing, so they have to keep gnawing and gnawing to wear their teeth down.

They are all rodents

There are more than 600 different kinds of mice.

MOUSE

House mice eat almost anything – even soap and glue!

Field mice prefer grains, fruit, insects and grass.

SQUIRREL

Most squirrels live in hollows in trees or in nests called dreys.

Their bushy tails help them balance in the treetops.

Squirrels bury nuts in the ground, then dig them up when food is scarce in winter.

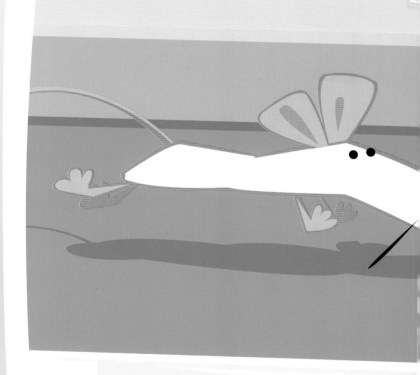

Mice can have many litters of babies each year – it doesn't take long for two mice to turn into two hundred!

VOLE

Voles dig out little runways or networks of **burrows** under grass and crops, so farmers and gardeners don't like them.

SQUEAK SQUEAK SQUEAK

Water voles live by rivers, lakes and ponds. If it gets too crowded, they have noisy, squeaky fights until one group moves out!

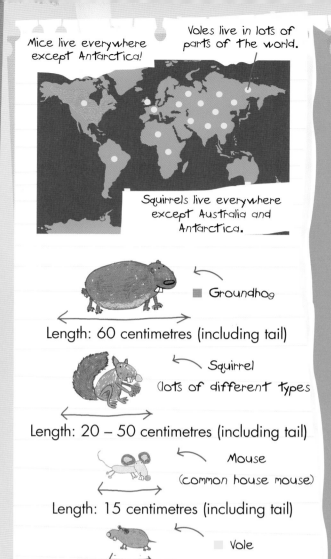

Mice live everywhere except Antarctica!

Voles live in lots of parts of the world.

Squirrels live everywhere except Australia and Antarctica.

Groundhog
Length: 60 centimetres (including tail)

Squirrel (lots of different types
Length: 20 – 50 centimetres (including tail)

Mouse (common house mouse)
Length: 15 centimetres (including tail)

Vole
Length: 10 – 20 centimetres (including tail)

GROUNDHOG

Groundhogs eat seeds, roots and plants. Their favourite food is clover.

Groundhogs dig long, deep burrows in empty fields.

In autumn, groundhogs eat a lot! They get very fat, ready to spend the winter in **hibernation**.

49

LIZARDS

Lizards are reptiles. They are related to snakes, but most lizards have legs, eyelids and ear openings.

CHAMELEON

Scaly with long tongues

KOMODO DRAGON

The chameleon's tongue is longer than its whole body!

When an insect or spider passes by, the chameleon flicks out its long, sticky tongue and catches it.

The chameleon can change colour to blend in with its background. This helps it hide from **predators** – and surprise its **prey**!

Each eye can move on its own. This means the chameleon can look in two different directions at once.

50

GECKO

Geckos can use their long tongues to clean their eyes.

Some geckos live around people. They are good pest controllers because they love eating bugs!

Geckos live in warm places.

Many geckos have tiny hairs on their feet – a bit like velcro. The hairs help them climb up walls.

Female Komodo dragons dig out large **burrows** in sandy ground to lay their eggs in. After the eggs have **hatched**, the babies live in trees to avoid predators.

Geckos are found on every continent except Antarctica.

Chameleons live in lots of places, too. Some are shown in yellow on the map.

Komodo dragon
Length: 3 metres

Chameleon
Length: 2.8 – 80 centimetres

Gecko
Length: up to 40 centimetres

The Komodo dragon can live to be 50 years old!

world's largest lizard

Komodo dragons can run fast. They travel long distances every day looking for their favourite food – the remains of dead animals.

Alligators and crocodiles live in warm, tropical places near rivers and **swamps**. Some crocodiles can live in seawater, too.

CROCODILE

A hungry crocodile can be very dangerous to people. Thankfully, once a crocodile has had a large meal, it won't need to eat again for several weeks!

The African crocodile bird picks out bits of food and dead **insects** from the crocodile's teeth and gums. The bird has a good meal, and the crocodile gets clean teeth.

Crocodiles and alligators eat fish, turtles, birds and mammals – even big ones! They can't chew, so they swallow small things whole.

52 To break up large **prey**, they hold it in their mouth and spin over and over in the water.

There are ways to tell crocodiles and alligators apart:
• Crocs have a long, narrow snout.
• Alligators have a wide snout.
• You can see a croc's lower teeth when its mouth is shut.
• When an alligator's mouth is shut, you can only see its upper teeth.

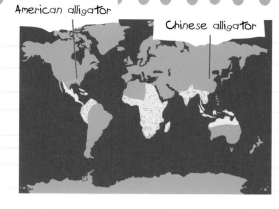

American alligator

Chinese alligator

Crocodile and alligator mums lay between 20 and 60 eggs at a time, in a waterside nest made from mud and leaves.

Crocodile

Length: up to 6 metres

Alligator

Length: up to 5 metres

They are very protective of their eggs and babies! When the eggs **hatch**, the mothers hear the babies calling and help them out of the nest.

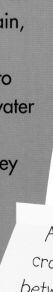

ALLIGATOR

During dry times when there is not much rain, alligators use their tails and hind legs to dig the last of the water from the bottom of waterholes. Then they lie in wait and catch the thirsty animals that come for a drink.

Alligators and crocodiles have between 60 and 80 teeth.

53

TURTLES AND TORTOISES

Turtles mainly live in the water, while tortoises live on land. They can both live to a very old age. There are records of tortoises living for more than 150 years!

The only reptiles with shells

TURTLE

A hawksbill turtle

Many turtles eat sea creatures like jellyfish, sea urchins and sea sponges. Others eat seaweed.

Turtles have **webbed** feet and a **streamlined** shell, to help them swim fast.

Most tortoises are **herbivores**. They eat grass and plants.

Turtles have a sharp beak for cutting their food, but no teeth.

Mother turtles dig nest holes on sandy beaches. They lay their eggs in the holes, bury them and then go back to sea.

When the eggs **hatch**, the babies have to look after themselves. They need to get to the sea fast, before they are spotted by **predators**.

IMPORTANT NOTE

Hawksbill turtles are critically **endangered**. They are hunted for their shells (for jewellery making) and the beaches where they lay their eggs are disturbed by the building of holiday hotels. Many other species of turtle are in great danger, too.

54

TORTOISE

Tortoise shells are high and domed. Their bodies store water and fat underneath the shell. Fat is also stored in their legs and tails.

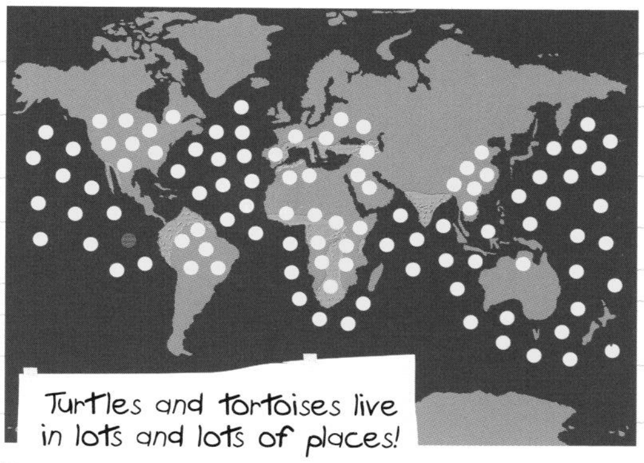

A dome-shaped shell

Turtles and tortoises live in lots and lots of places!

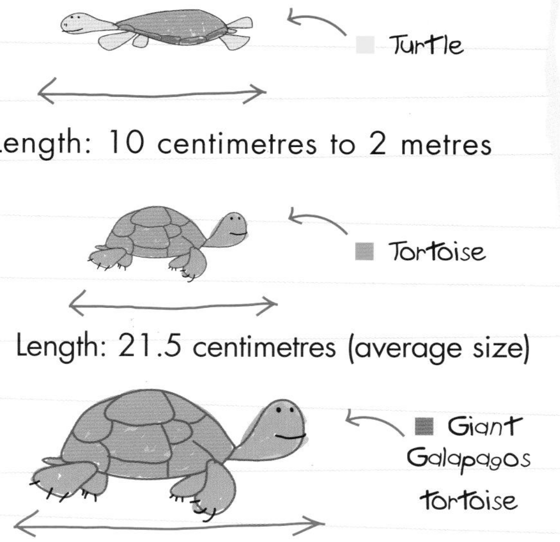

Turtle

Length: 10 centimetres to 2 metres

Tortoise

Length: 21.5 centimetres (average size)

Giant Galapagos tortoise

Length: up to 1.3 metres

Desert tortoises live in underground **burrows**. They can go for up to a year without water. They get all the moisture they need from the grass and wild flowers they eat in the spring.

If they live in a place that gets cold in winter, some tortoises will **hibernate** for several months.

55

SNAKES

Snakes are cold-blooded reptiles with no legs. Most snakes cannot see or hear very well, but they have a good **sense** of smell. Some snakes use their tongues to 'taste' the air for the scent of their **prey**.

PYTHON

Pythons wrap their coils around their prey. Each time the trapped animal breathes out, the python tightens its grip until its victim stops breathing. Then the python swallows it – head first!

The reticulated python is the world's longest snake. It can grow to 8 metres long and weigh 200 kilograms!

This is an African royal python, or ball python.

A group of snake eggs is called a 'clutch'. Pythons lay between 10 and 100 eggs at a time.

56 The reticulated python can swallow an animal as big as a deer – WHOLE!

COBRA

The king cobra is the world's biggest **venomous** snake.

Cobras have 'hoods' of skin. They spread them to make themselves look bigger and extra scary.

Some cobras spit their **venom** at their prey (birds, small mammals, lizards and other snakes), but most use their **fangs** to inject venom into their victims.

Some cobras would be able to kill an elephant with a single bite!

Pythons, cobras and rattlesnakes live in lots of places – some are shown here.

Royal python   King cobra

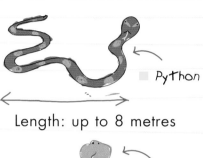

Python

Length: up to 8 metres

Cobra

Length: up to 4 metres

Rattlesnake

Length: up to 2.5 metres

RATTLESNAKE

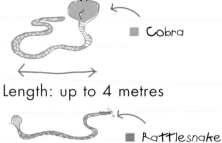

Rattlesnakes inject small animals with venom from their fangs, and then swallow them whole!

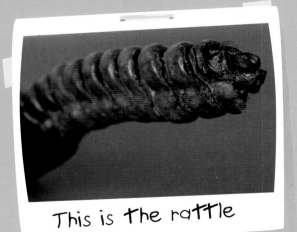

This is the rattle

The rattlesnake's rattle is made of sections of hard skin at the end of its tail. The rattle warns enemies not to come near.

Like all snakes, rattlesnakes shed their skin from time to time. Each time this happens, a new section is added to their rattle.

57

FROGS, TOADS and others

Most amphibians live part of their life in water and part on land. They take in moisture through their skin, so they don't have to drink water.

These are all amphibians

FROG

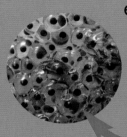
Most frogs and toads lay their eggs in water. Toads lay their eggs in long strings, while frogs lay eggs in clusters, called frogspawn.

The baby frogs, called tadpoles, **hatch** from the frogspawn in a few days.

EUROPEAN
COMMON
FROG

Frogspawn

4 weeks old

12 weeks old

16 weeks old
Grown-up!

It normally takes just a few months for them to turn into frogs.

Some frogs have brightly coloured skin to warn **predators** that they are poisonous.

58 The South American poison arrow frog's skin is so deadly that local people use the poison for their arrow tips!

Frogs catch **insects** on their long, sticky tongues. Toads like to eat insects, too – and SLUGS!

TOAD

Toads are similar to frogs, but have drier, bumpier skin.

Their back legs are shorter, too.

Newts and salamanders live in lots of places. Some of them are shown here.

Toads and frogs can be found on every continent except Antarctica.

 Frog

Length: 1 – 40 centimetres

 Toad

Length: 2 – 25 centimetres

 ■ Newt

Length: 6 – 30 centimetres

Salamander

Length: 6 – 35 centimetres

SALAMANDER

Salamanders and newts look like lizards, but they don't have scales and they are amphibians.

Most salamanders hide under rocks and leaves during the day and come out at night to feed on insects, worms and snails.

A fire salamander

The giant salamander, which lives in China, is the biggest in the world – it can grow to 1.5 metres long.

59

FISH

Fish live in both salt and **freshwater** all over the world. They can even breathe underwater! They suck in water through their mouths, then push it out through special slits called **gills**. The gills help the fish get oxygen out of the water.

GOLDFISH

If goldfish are kept in an indoor aquarium, they stay quite small. But if they live in a pond or stream, where they have lots of room to move about, they can grow to be 25 centimetres long!

Goldfish are not only gold. They can be silvery white, red, greenish-brown and even black.

FLYING FISH

To escape from **predators** (like dolphins) the flying fish flaps its tail from side to side to build up speed, then whizzes up to the water's surface. Then it launches itself into the air and then glides on its outstretched fins for nearly 500 metres.

Flying fish don't have wings. They have special, large fins.

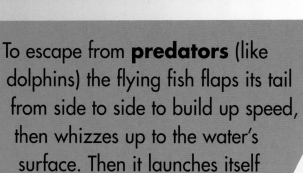

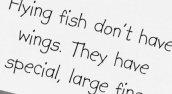

60

X-RAY FISH

X-ray fish live in lakes and rivers. They lay hundreds of tiny eggs among the underwater plants.

X-ray fish eat **insects** and **plankton**.

The tiny x-ray fish gets its name from its see-through body!

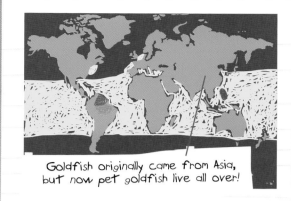

Goldfish originally came from Asia, but now pet goldfish live all over!

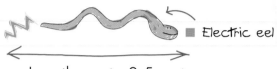
■ Electric eel

Length: up to 2.5 metres

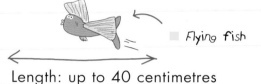
Flying fish

Length: up to 40 centimetres

Goldfish

Length: 7.5 centimetres (average)

■ Tomato clownfish

Length: 5 – 14 centimetres

■ X-ray fish

Length: 5 centimetres

CLOWNFISH

The clownfish lives on **coral reefs** hidden from predators among the stinging tentacles of sea anemones.

Its body is covered in a special slime which scientists believe help to protect the fish from the anemone's stings.

Clownfish eat plankton and **algae**.

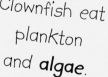

ELECTRIC EEL

Unlike most fish the electric eel doesn't have scales or gills. It comes to the surface to breathe.

Their bodies produce electricity to stun their **prey**. They can even produce a HUGE jolt of electricity that can kill a fish – or a person!

61

SHARKS

These fearsome-looking, meat-eating fish live all over the world, mostly in warm seas. People believe that sharks attack humans all the time, but actually there are fewer than 100 shark attacks a year.

GREAT WHITE SHARK

The great white shark has a very good **sense** of smell and is an excellent hunter. It can smell just one drop of blood in 94 litres of water! Its favourite foods are seals, sea lions, dolphins and other sharks – but it will eat any creature it can catch!

Some sharks give birth to live babies, called pups. The pups have teeth and start to hunt right away! Great white shark pups are over a metre long when they're born.

Great white sharks have LOTS of teeth. They grow in rows with new ones replacing old ones all the time. A great white shark may grow more than 20,000 new teeth in its lifetime.

A shark's skeleton is made of cartilage, the same bendy stuff that's in your ears and nose!

62

WHALE SHARK

The GIANT whale shark only eats tiny plants and animals called **plankton**.

The whale shark is the biggest fish in the

It swims along slowly, filtering the plankton from the water through its **gills**.

■ Whale shark

Length: up to 14 metres

■ Great white shark

Length: 3.5 – 5 metres

■ Hammerhead shark

Length: 3.5 metres

HAMMERHEAD SHARK

The hammerhead's weird head is actually very useful – it helps the shark steer through the water and sense movement around it.

With an eye and a nostril at each end of the 'hammer', it can find food over a wider area.

Hammerheads eat fish, squid – and sometimes other sharks!

63

INSIDE OUT ANIMALS

These amazing creatures are called **crustaceans**, and they all have their skeletons on the outsides of their bodies! Crustaceans mainly live in the sea, but some live in **freshwater** and even on land.

They have **antennae** and bodies in three sections

LOBSTER

Lobsters use their tail and their five pairs of legs for swimming.

Their huge front legs are snapping claws that they use to defend themselves.

Lobsters crawl along the seabed at night. They eat dead animals and sometimes fish and small sea creatures.

Lobsters can live to be 50 years old.

SHRIMP

Shrimps have five pairs of walking legs and five pairs of swimming legs.

HERMIT CRAB

No place like home!

Unlike other crustaceans, hermit crabs don't have their own shells. They use the empty shells of snails or other animals.

Hermit crabs that live near land may even move into coconut shells!

When it gets too big for its home, the hermit crab leaves its shell and moves to a larger one.

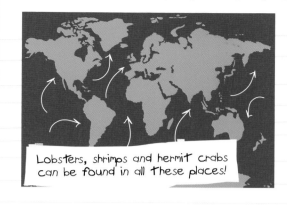

Lobsters, shrimps and hermit crabs can be found in all these places!

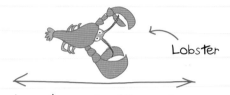
Lobster
Length: up to 45 centimetres

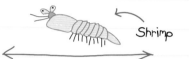
Shrimp
Length: 1.6 – 20 centimetres

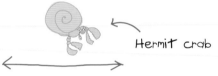
Hermit crab
Length: 12 centimetres

Shrimps live on the floor of oceans and lakes. They eat plants and other small creatures.

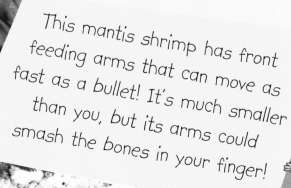

This mantis shrimp has front feeding arms that can move as fast as a bullet! It's much smaller than you, but its arms could smash the bones in your finger!

Shrimps always swim backwards. To swim, they push their abdomen (the middle bit of their body) in and out and whip their tail from side to side.

Shrimps lay up to 14,000 eggs at a time. The eggs stay attached to the female's legs until they are ready to **hatch**.

UNDERWATER ODDITIES

Some of the strangest-looking creatures on Earth live under the sea.

The giant octopus can grow to 10 metres across.

OCTOPUS

Octopuses have eight arm-like tentacles. If they lose a tentacle, they just grow a new one!

When a **predator** attacks, the octopus squirts out a black, inky liquid. This makes the water cloudy so the octopus can escape.

Octopus like to eat fish, crabs, lobsters and shellfish.

These suckers help it hold on to **prey**.

JELLYFISH

Its mouth is under here.

SAWFISH

Sawfish use their snouts to dig up their prey. Their long, toothy snouts look just like saws.

Sometimes sawfish slash at schools of fish. Then they collect up any dead or injured fish from the seabed.

FLOUNDER

When a flounder is born, it has an eye on each side of its head and looks like a normal fish.

After a few days, the fish starts tipping over and swimming on one side. The eye that is underneath moves around to the top side, so both eyes are on the same side!

Baby flounders live near the surface of the sea. When they are grown-up, flounders live on the seabed searching for small fish to eat.

Jellyfish have no brains, hearts or bones. They are just made of muscles, nerves and water!

These tentacles can sting! They help the jellyfish catch its dinner of fish.

Jellyfish bodies are see-through, so you can see what they've had for dinner!

Octopus and jellyfish can be found in all these places.

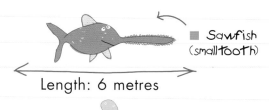

■ Sawfish (smalltooth)

Length: 6 metres

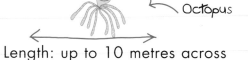

Octopus

Length: up to 10 metres across

Flounder

Length: up to 94 centimetres

Jellyfish

Length: can be up to 18 metres including tentacles!

■ Seahorse

Length: up to 19 centimetres

SEAHORSE

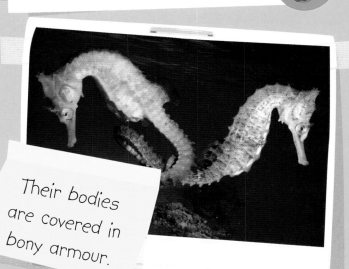

Their bodies are covered in bony armour.

Seahorses are actually fish. They eat **plankton**.

Male seahorses help give birth to their babies. The female lays the eggs in a pouch on the male's front. Dad carries the eggs until they are ready to **hatch**.

67

ANTS

Ants are found all over the world, except for Antarctica. Some are meat-eaters, others eat plants and a few only drink honeydew made by bugs. Most ants cannot see, instead they release special smells so they can signal to each other! Ants live in big **colonies**, like a huge family.

Looks a bit crowded!

Most of the ants in a colony are 'workers'. Inside the nest, some workers look after the eggs (which are laid by the queen ant), while others collect food to feed the **larvae**. Some ants are 'soldiers', they defend the nest.

68

Ants can't swallow solid food so they squeeze out the liquid from the food instead.

Hold on tight!

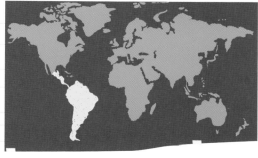
There are ants living in all parts of the world – except the very coldest bits!

→ Army ant
Length: up to 1 centimetre

→ Black garden ant
Length: up to 4 millimetres

Ants can lift 20 times their own body weight.

Ants have a stomach (for food for themselves) and a 'crop' (a special place inside them) where they can store food to share with the other ants.

Ants are very fast runners. If an ant was the same size as a human it could run as fast as a racehorse!

Ants can be very clean and tidy. Some ants have a separate chamber in their nest to put waste in. This keeps it away from the rest of the nest.

It's a good job they're not this BIG!

69

HAIRY SPIDERS

You may think spiders are **insects,** but they are actually different creatures, called **arachnids**. There are about 40,000 different types of spider, and they all make silk inside their bodies. Some spiders use the silk to make traps called webs.

Eight eyes and eight legs.

JUMPING SPIDER

Long-jump champs!

Jumping spiders are very hairy and often brightly coloured.

Like all spiders, jumping spiders have eight eyes. Two of them are very big, like car headlights.

Jumping spiders can leap up to 25 times the length of their body – that would be like you jumping the length of five cars!

70 The spider's big eyes help it spot the insects it likes to eat from a long way off.

This web is called an orb web. You will often see spiders that build orb webs in the garden.

ORB WEB SPIDER

Orb web spiders build circular webs. The spider waits in the centre, and when it feels vibrations (little movements) with its feet, it knows that an insect (like a fly) has come into the web.

The spider rushes out and grabs its **prey**. It wraps it in silk thread – then it's dinnertime!

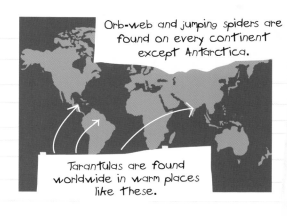

Orb-web and jumping spiders are found on every continent except Antarctica.

Tarantulas are found worldwide in warm places like these.

Body: up to 12 centimetres across

Tarantula

Leg span: up to 28 centimetres

Orb web spider

Body: 2.5 centimetres across

Jumping spider

Body: 1 centimetre across

TARANTULA

Some tarantulas nest in **burrows** dug into the earth, while others live in trees.

Tarantulas eat insects, frogs, lizards, mice and sometimes birds.

Tarantulas are the biggest of all the spiders.

Tarantulas crush their prey with their **fangs**, then dribble special juices over the dead body. The juices turn the creature into a liquid that can be sucked up!

They can also use their fangs to inject **venom** into their prey.

71

FLYING INSECTS

You don't just *see* **insects** busying about on the ground – you can *see* them flying about, too!

Butterflies and moths look alike, but butterflies are usually more colourful. Butterflies are active during the day, while most moths are only active at night.

BUTTERFLY

Butterflies and moths both have four life stages:
1) They start off as eggs. 2) Caterpillars hatch out of the eggs. 3) The caterpillars make themselves a cosy shell called a 'pupa'. 4) Inside the pupa the caterpillar turns into a butterfly or moth. 5) The butterfly or moth comes out of the pupa and flies away!

Many butterflies can taste with their feet! If a leaf will make tasty food for their babies (the caterpillars), they lay their eggs on it.

FIREFLY

The underside of the firefly's stomach has a special part that lights up.

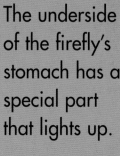

Special patterns of flashes help fireflies find **mates**. They also warn other fireflies of danger and let **predators** know that they taste nasty!

HONEYBEE

Honeybees live in **colonies** in special bee homes called hives.

Inside they build little waxy sections called 'cells'. The queen bee lays an egg in each cell. The eggs grow into **larvae**, and then the larvae become bees.

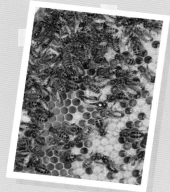

Worker bees collect **nectar** from flowers. They eat the sweet nectar and turn it into honey inside their bodies. The bee larvae are fed on honey.

Butterflies, dragonflies and honeybees can be found in every part of the world!

Fireflies are found all over the world, but especially in these places.

Butterfly
Wingspan: 1.7 – 15 centimetres

Dragonfly
Wingspan: 2 – 16 centimetres

Honeybee
Length: 1.2 centimetres

Firefly
Length: 0.5 – 2.5 centimetres

DRAGONFLY

Dragonflies live near lakes, ponds and streams. They can fly faster than 65 km/h to catch the small flying insects they eat.

They breathe through holes in their stomachs.

Their huge, bulging eyes can see in all directions.

Young dragonflies are called nymphs. They live under the water.

73

WORMS AND BEETLES

You've probably seen some of these 'creepy crawlies' in a park or in your garden. They work hard, getting rid of pests and rubbish, and helping things to grow.

STAG BEETLE

Stag beetles fighting

Male stag beetles have jaws shaped like a stag's **antlers**. The males use their antlers when they are fighting over females.

Stag beetles are the biggest beetles in Europe. They eat rotting wood and sap (a sticky liquid inside trees).

IMPORTANT NOTE

Stag beetles need rotting wood to eat, but the forests where they live are being cut down. There used to be lots of stag beetles all over the world – now they are endangered.

If a bird comes too close to a ladybird it will 'play dead'. Many birds won't eat an insect that isn't moving!

When the weather gets cold, ladybirds keep warm by huddling together in groups of up to 100. In winter they **hibernate**.

74

LADYBIRD

Farmers and gardeners love ladybirds, because they eat aphids, little bugs that damage plants.

The hard shell protects their wings and the bright red colour warns birds that they taste bad!

Any aphids to eat?

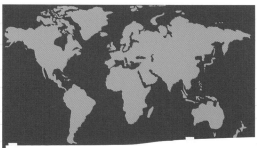

The earthworm, stag beetle and ladybird can be found on every continent except Antarctica.

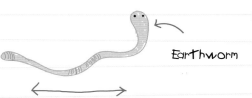
Earthworm

Length: up to 25 centimetres

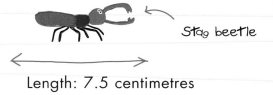
Stag beetle

Length: 7.5 centimetres

Ladybird

Length: 9 millimetres

EARTHWORM

Earthworms eat rotting leaves and dead bits of plants. They will also eat the rotting remains of animals.

Earthworms cannot see or hear, but they can feel vibrations (small movements).

Wriggly worms

One type of earthworm in Australia can grow to 3.3 metres long!

Their waste (or poo) is called castings. The castings are filled with nutrients (goodness) which goes back into the soil and helps to feed plants.

75

SEA BIRDS

All these birds are at home on the sea, but they come ashore to build nests and lay their eggs. Penguin mums and dads take turns sitting on the nest or looking for food. Seagulls nest on high, rocky cliffs or rooftops. Albatrosses set up nesting **colonies** on remote islands where there are no people.

PENGUINS

Penguins eat fish, squid and **crustaceans**.

Penguins can't fly and they are clumsy on land. But they are very quick and graceful in the water.

Sometimes penguins toboggan across the snow on their bellies – it's easier than walking!

Super swimmers

A layer of **blubber** keeps penguins warm.

There may be thousands of baby penguins in a colony, but parents always recognize their own chick by its voice.

These emperor penguins live on the Antarctic ice. The male keeps the egg warm on his feet – under his belly. The egg **hatches** after about two months.

ALBATROSS

Sailors used to believe that killing an albatross would bring bad luck.

The wandering albatross has the longest wingspan of any bird – 3.5 metres!

Albatrosses like windy weather. Their long wings make them excellent gliders, and they can float in the air for hours, without ever flapping their wings. They only come ashore to breed.

Their favourite foods are fish and squid.

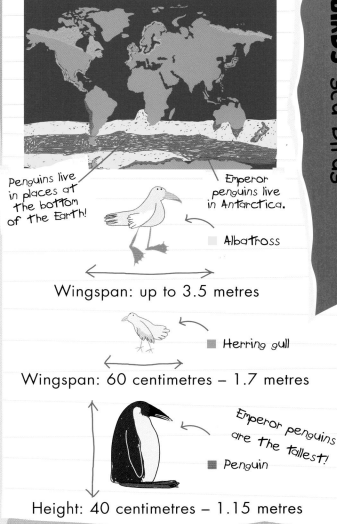

Penguins live in places at the bottom of the Earth!

Emperor penguins live in Antarctica.

Albatross

Wingspan: up to 3.5 metres

Herring gull

Wingspan: 60 centimetres – 1.7 metres

Emperor penguins are the tallest!

Penguin

Height: 40 centimetres – 1.15 metres

SEAGULL

At sea, gulls dive for fish, but closer to the shore they pick up crustaceans and **insects** on beaches.

Herring gulls scavenge for food in rubbish close to the shore. This can help keep bays and harbours clean, but in some places there are so many gulls that they become a nuisance.

77

HUNTING BIRDS

Birds that hunt other animals for food are called 'birds of prey'. Owls and eagles both use their strong claws to grab and kill their **prey**.

OWL

With their soft feathers, owls make no noise when they fly.

Most owls are **nocturnal**. They hunt for mice and other small mammals at night.

Owls have better hearing than any other bird. They also have very good eyesight and can turn their heads almost all the way round. This helps them to see all around them.

78

The bald eagle is the national bird of the USA.

BALD EAGLE

The big, powerful bald eagle is not really bald – the white feathers on its head make it look bald from far away.

Bald eagles nest in high, hard-to-reach places. They use the same nest over and over, adding more branches and twigs every year. The largest bald eagle nest ever found was 6.1 metres deep and 2.9 metres wide!

Bald eagles usually live near water. They grab fish from the surface with their claws. They also eat other birds, small mammals, reptiles and carrion (dead animals).

Owls can be found everywhere in the world except Antarctica.

Wingspan: 2.25 metres

Height: 1 metre

■ Bald eagle

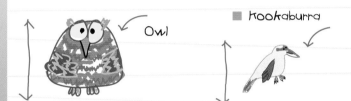

Owl

■ kookaburra

Height: 14 – 70 centimetres

Height: 43 centimetres

KOOKABURRA

Kookaburras use their loud, shrieking call to tell other kookaburras where they are. It sounds like they are laughing.

Ha ha ha!

They eat **insects**, worms and reptiles – even poisonous snakes.

Young kookaburras often help raise their younger brothers and sisters.

79

BIRDS THAT LOVE WATER

Birds like ducks, swans and geese are called waterfowl. They have webbed feet for swimming and their bodies produce special water-repellent oils which the birds spread through their feathers.

CANADA GOOSE

The female Canada goose builds a nest on the ground, near water. The gander (male) stands guard.

wait for us mum!

The goslings (babies) grow very quickly.

Canada geese eat grass, seeds and plants.

In autumn, Canada geese fly south to spend the winter in warmer places. They fly in a 'V' shape, honking as they go!

The lead bird in the 'V' creates a slipstream – a stream of air that helps to pull all the other birds along. When the lead bird gets tired, one from the back, who has had a rest, takes over.

80

SWAN

Swans are the fastest swimmers and fastest flyers of all the waterfowl. They eat plants and small underwater creatures.

Biggest waterfowl

Baby swans are called cygnets. They have short necks and fluffy brown or grey feathers.

Just like in the story the 'Ugly Duckling'. It takes a year or two before cygnets turn white.

Cobs (males) and pens (females) pair up and stay together their whole lives.

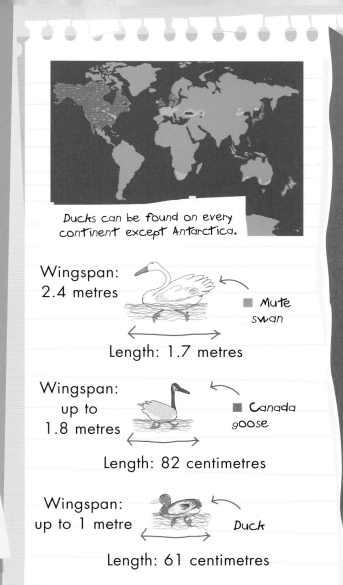

Ducks can be found on every continent except Antarctica.

Wingspan: 2.4 metres

Length: 1.7 metres

Mute swan

Wingspan: up to 1.8 metres

Length: 82 centimetres

Canada goose

Wingspan: up to 1 metre

Length: 61 centimetres

Duck

DUCKS

The mallard is the wild relative of most **domestic** ducks. The males have colourful feathers, while the females are completely brown.

Most domestic ducks are white. Males and females look almost the same.

Eiders and scoters are diving ducks. They live on the sea and eat shellfish and **crustaceans.**

Mallards eat plants, insects, frogs, worms, snails and slugs!

81

BIRDS WITH SPECIAL TALENTS

All birds can do amazing things, but these unusual birds have skills that make them extra-special!

Good at pecking and running!

UMBRELLABIRD

The umbrellabird lives in tall rainforest trees. It likes to eat fruit.

 When a male umbrellabird wants to attract a **mate**, he spreads out the tuft of feathers on his head. It looks just like an umbrella!

Umbrellabirds also have 'wattles'. These are folds of skin that hang from their throats.

IMPORTANT NOTE

The umbrellabird is in danger because it is losing its habitat. The rainforest trees that it lives in are being cut down by people who want to sell the wood, or who need to clear the land so that they can grow food.

ROADRUNNER

Roadrunners eat lizards, snakes, birds and small animals – they spear them with their beaks!

Long legs make roadrunners very speedy. They race along at up to 25 Km/h.

82

WOODPECKER

Most woodpeckers peck holes in trees to find **insects** to eat.

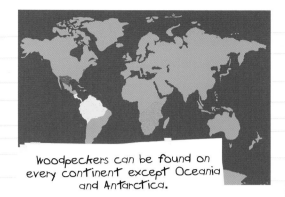

Woodpeckers can be found on every continent except Oceania and Antarctica.

Their stiff tail feathers and strong feet keep them upright while they peck at tree trunks.

■ Roadrunner

Length: 58 centimetres

Height: 48 centimetres

Umbrellabird

Woodpecker

Length: 13 – 60 centimetres

When roadrunners sense danger, they crouch and try to hide. But if they need to escape from a **predator**, they can make a fast getaway.

■ Oxpecker bird

Length: 22 centimetres

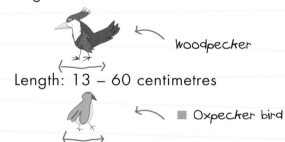

Their long, narrow tails help the birds to balance while they're running. And they help them to make speedy turns.

OXPECKER BIRD

Oxpeckers are also called tick-birds.

They eat the ticks and flies that annoy big mammals such as cattle, rhinos and elephants.

Their sharp claws help them to cling on to the animals' backs.

When two creatures help each other in this way, they are called **symbionts**.

83

BIRDS THAT SING

Most birds sing to attract a **mate**, or to tell other birds where their **territory** is. The mockingbird copies the songs of other birds and can even make sounds like a dog barking and piano music!

Popstars of the bird world!

NIGHTINGALE

A shy nightingale

Nightingales mainly sing at night. Their song is loud with a beautiful tune, but they are quite shy – so it is hard to spot them.

When males are trying to find a mate, they sing all day and all night. They only stop singing when a female joins them.

Nightingales eat **insects**, worms, spiders, berries and fruit.

They build bowl-shaped nests made of twigs and grass.

84 Nightingales nest near the ground. Their nests are made of twigs and lined with grass.

CARDINAL

Male and female cardinals sing to each other all year long. They are especially loud just before nesting time, in the spring.

The male cardinal is easy to spot with his bright red feathers. Females have some red feathers too, but they are mostly dull brown and grey.

Cardinals like to eat seeds, insects, snails and the sap (sticky juice) from maple trees.

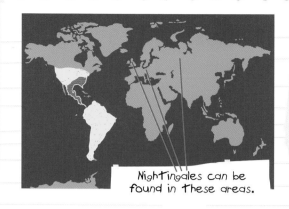

Nightingales can be found in these areas.

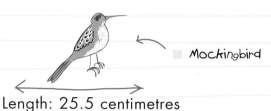
Mockingbird
Length: 25.5 centimetres

Cardinal
Length: 22 centimetres

Nightingale
Length: 16.5 centimetres

MOCKINGBIRD

Tough mums!

Mockingbirds can sing for hours at a time.

Mother mockingbirds are so protective they will even attack cats or people if they think their eggs or babies are in danger.

They like to eat fruit, grasshoppers, beetles, spiders, lizards and snakes!

85

BIG BIRDS

Some birds are taller than you! Ostriches are even bigger than your mum and dad – they are the world's biggest birds.

OSTRICH

Ostriches cannot fly, but to escape a **predator** they can run very fast – up to 70 km/h.

The ostrich's long, thin neck makes up almost half its height.

Ostriches live in large herds, searching for their favourite foods – plants and grass.

Several females in a herd will share a nest, and lay their eggs together.

Ostrich eggs are about the size of a honeydew melon – the biggest egg in the animal kingdom.

86 When the eggs **hatch**, dad looks after the babies.

FLAMINGO

Flamingos live in huge flocks in wetlands (places where there is lots of shallow water). Sometimes there can be one million birds in a flock!

The American flamingo's pink colour comes from the shrimp they eat. Without it, their feathers would turn white.

Flamingos can stand on one leg for ages, even when they're asleep! This stops them losing too much heat from their legs and feet.

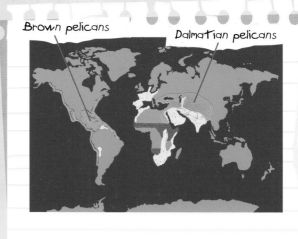

Brown pelicans   Dalmatian pelicans

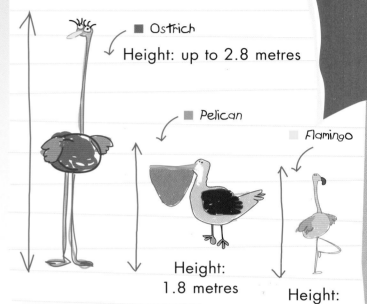

■ Ostrich
Height: up to 2.8 metres

■ Pelican

■ Flamingo

Height: 1.8 metres

Height: 1.4 metres

PELICAN

Pelicans have a big, stretchy throat pouch. They scoop up lots of water in the pouch, then strain out the liquid, and swallow any fish that are left inside.

Dalmatian pelicans fish in groups. They form a line and chase small fish into shallow water – then they scoop them up.

The North American brown pelican dives straight down into the sea to catch fish.

87

COLOURFUL BIRDS

With their brilliantly coloured feathers, these birds stand out from the rest of the flock!

PEAFOWL

HUMMINGBIRD

Hummingbird wings beat extremely fast. This allows the bird to hover over flowers. The bird positions its long, specially shaped beak in the flower and licks out the **nectar** with its long tongue.

They blend in with the flowers, making it hard for **predators** to see them.

Hummingbirds are the smallest birds in the world!

Only the peacocks (male peafowl) have a long and colourful tail.

PARROT

This colourful scarlet macaw lives high in the rainforest treetops. It can live to be 80 years old.

IMPORTANT NOTE
*Many parrots are **endangered**. Their forest homes are cut down, and they are captured to be sold as pets!*

88

All parrots have strong, hooked beaks and muscular tongues that they use to break into fruits and seeds. They eat nectar and **insects** too.

Peafowl eat seeds, fruit, plants, insects and sometimes small creatures such as mice. They feed on the ground, but sleep in trees.

BLUEBIRD

In some parts of North America, the arrival of the bluebird from its winter home in the south is a sure sign that spring is coming.

Bluebirds build their nests in holes in trees or fences.

They feed on butterflies, beetles, spiders and small insects.

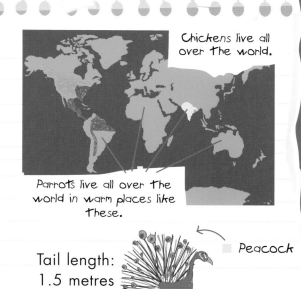

Chickens live all over the world.

Parrots live all over the world in warm places like these.

Peacock
Tail length: 1.5 metres
Body length: 1.1 metres

Parrot
Length: up to 1 metre

Bluebird
Length: 18 centimetres

Chicken
Height: 66 centimetres

Hummingbird
Length: 5.5 centimetres

CHICKEN

 comb

 wattles

Cockerels (male chickens) are more brightly coloured than hens (females).

They have a larger comb and wattles, and long tail feathers, too.

'cock-a-doodle-doo'

The peacock displays his tail in a wide fan when he wants to attract a peahen (female).

The cockerel's cry attracts females and warns other males that he is around!

89

SCAVENGER BIRDS

They eat leftovers!

Scavengers are birds (or other animals) that eat whatever they can find! Some scavengers eat carrion – the remains of animals or birds that have died or been killed by another animal.

CITY PIGEON

City pigeons nest on bridges or buildings, and in little holes or on ledges.

Speedy pigeons can fly at 100 km/h. That's the speed of a car on a motorway! Wild pigeons are not normally scavengers.

But city pigeons eat leftover food they find on pavements and in parks.

City pigeons are descended from rock doves – wild pigeons that nests on cliffs.

CROW

Crows like to eat carrion, but also fruit, **insects** and grain in farmers' fields!

RAVEN

Ravens are the biggest members of the crow family. With their glossy blue-black feathers, black feet and large beaks, ravens look very scary.

They eat almost anything, including seeds, berries and rubbish!

Ravens are very clever. Young birds can sometimes be taught to copy human speech.

Some farmers put up scarecrows to 'scare crows' away from their crops.

Sometimes crows live in huge flocks. While they eat, one or two look-outs keep watch for danger.

Crows live everywhere except Antarctica and some parts of Oceania.

Ravens live in Europe, Asia, North America and North Africa.

Pigeons live on every continent except Antarctica.

Vulture
Length: up to 1.3 metres

Raven
Length: 66 centimetres

Crow
Length: 45 centimetres

Pigeon
Length: 34 centimetres

VULTURE

Vultures sometimes hunt live **prey**, but mostly they help themselves to other animals' leftovers!

Their strong beaks are good at tearing up skin and flesh.

91

GLOSSARY

ALGAE Types of simple plants. Algae have no stems, flowers or leaves (e.g. pond scum).

ANTENNAE A pair of movable feelers on the head of an insect or crustacean.

ANTLERS A pair of horn-like growths on the heads of some deer. Antlers sometimes look like tree branches!

AQUATIC An animal or bird that lives most or all of its life in or on the water.

ARACHNIDS Creatures with four pairs of legs. Members of this family include spiders and ticks.

BLOWHOLES Openings on the top of the head that cetaceans (aquatic mammals) use to breathe through when they come to the surface.

BLUBBER A thick layer of fat under the skin that keeps an animal warm.

BURROWS Holes or tunnels that an animal digs in the ground as its home, or to use as a shelter.

CAMOUFLAGE Colourings or markings on an animal that help it hide or blend in with its surroundings. Camouflage is a good way to hide from predators, and a good way to stop prey from seeing you coming!

CARNIVORES Animals that only eat meat or fish.

CETACEANS Aquatic mammals (like whales and dolphins) that live underwater, but need to come to the surface to breathe.

COLONIES Groups of animals that live together.

CORAL REEFS Huge, underwater places that look as if they are made from rocks, but are actually made from the bodies of coral animals called polyps. The polyps have hard outer skeletons that all join together. When a polyp dies, its skeleton stays as part of the reef, so the reefs keep on getting bigger and bigger.

CRUSTACEANS Aquatic animals, like lobsters and crabs. They have a hard, outer shell, instead of a skeleton, and bodies in sections with jointed legs.

DOMESTIC Animals that live with people. Pets and farm animals are domestic animals.

ENDANGERED When there are not many of an animal left, and the remaining animals are in danger of being hunted by humans or losing their habitat (the place where they live).

FANGS Very sharp teeth used by mammals for grabbing prey and tearing meat. Snakes' fangs are hollow (like little tubes) and are used to inject venom.

FRESHWATER Rainwater and the water in lakes, ponds, rivers and streams. It is not salty.

GILLS Special organs in the bodies of fish and some amphibians (normally near the head). The gills take oxygen out of the water and send it into the fish's body so that it can breathe.

HATCH To be born by breaking out of an egg.

HERBIVORES Animals that only eat plants.

HIBERNATION Spending most or all of the winter sleeping, while food is scarce. Hibernating animals live off their body fat. Many of the animals in this book hibernate: *grizzly bear; hedgehog; skunk; some bats (ones that live in places that are cold in winter); white-tailed prairie dog; some mice; groundhog; turtle; tortoise; rattlesnake; frog; toad; newt; salamander; goldfish (if kept outdoors); honeybee; ladybird.*

INSECTS Tiny creatures with bodies in three sections and three pairs of legs. Many insects have wings, too.

LARVAE The young of many kinds of insects.

MARINE Having to do with the sea. Marine mammals are mammals that live in the sea.

MARSUPIALS Animals best known for carrying their newborn babies in a pouch (pocket) outside their body until the babies are big enough to look after themselves.

MATES When a male and female animal come together to produce babies. The word used for an animal's partner (its mate).

NECTAR A sweet liquid made by plants. Bees use it to make honey, and many other insects and birds eat it.

NOCTURNAL When an animal is only active at night.

OMNIVORES Animals that eat meat (or fish) and plants.

PLANKTON Microscopic (very, very tiny) plants and animals that live in the sea and in lakes.

PREDATORS Animals that hunt and kill other animals for food.

PREY An animal that is hunted and killed by another animal for food.

PRIMATES An animal group that includes monkeys and apes. Humans are primates, too.

SCENT GLANDS Organs (parts) of an animal's body that give out a smelly scent.

SENSES Hearing, seeing, smelling, tasting and touching – the way animals get information from the world around them.

STREAMLINED When something is a smooth shape and is therefore able to move faster through the air or water because there is no resistance.

SWAMPS Very wet areas with lots of water plants.

SYMBIONTS Animals from different species that live together and help each other.

TERRITORY The area which one animal defends against other animals, to keep its food supply and family safe.

TUSKS Very long, pointed teeth that grow out of an animal's face or mouth.

VENOM A poison produced in the bodies of some animals, such as snakes and spiders.

VENOMOUS The word used to describe an animal that produces venom.

WEBBED Feet where the toes are joined together by a flap of skin.

ANIMAL BABY NAMES

Alligator: hatchling

Anteater: young/baby

Antelope: calf

Ape: infant/young

Armadillo: young/baby

Bald eagle: eaglet

Bat: no special name

Bear: cub

Beaver: kit/pup

Bird (*Albatross; bluebird; cardinal; chicken; crow; flamingo; kookaburra; hummingbird; mocking bird; nightingale; ostrich; oxpecker bird; parrot; pelican; penguin; raven; seagull; umbrellabird; vulture; woodpecker*): chick

Butterfly: caterpillar

Camel: calf

Cheetah: cub

Cow: calf

Crab: larva

Crocodile: hatchling

Dolphin: calf

Domestic dog: puppy

Dragonfly: nymph

Duck: duckling

Earthworm: no special name

Electric eel: elver

Elephant: calf

Firefly: larva

Fish: fry/minnow

Flying squirrel: pup

Fox: cub/kit

Frog: tadpole

Giraffe: calf

Goat: kid

Goose: gosling

Groundhog: kit/cub

Hedgehog: piglet

Hippopotamus: calf

Honeybee: larva

Horse: foal

Ibex: kid

Jack rabbit (*hare*): leveret

Jellyfish: juvenile medusa

Kangaroo: joey

Koala: joey

Ladybird: larva

Leopard: cub

Lion: cub

Lizard: no special name

Lobster: larva

Manatee: calf

Monkeys: infant

Moose (*elk*): calf

Mouse: kitten

Octopus: no special name

Owl: owlet/howlet

Peafowl: pea-chick

Pig: piglet

Pigeon: squab

Platypus: puggle

Porcupine: porcupette

Prairie dog: young

Rabbit: kitten/bunny

Raccoon: kit/cub

Reindeer: fawn

Rhinoceros: calf

Ring-tailed lemur: infant

Salamander: larva

Sea lion: pup

Sea otter: pup/

kitten/cub

Seahorse: sea ponies

Seal: pup

Shark: pup

Shrimp: larva

Skunk: kitten

Sloth: young/baby

Snake: no special name

Spider: spiderling

Squirrel: pup

Stag beetle: grub

Swan: cygnet

Tasmanian Devil: cub

Tiger: cub

Toad: tadpole

Tortoise: hatchling

Turtle: hatchling

Vole: no special name

Walrus: cub

Whale: calf

Wild boar: boarlet/piglet

Wolf: cub

Yak: calf

Zebra: foal/colt

INDEX

95

INDEX

PICTURE CREDITS